A SLICE OF **GOLF**

A SLICE OF **GOLF**

MARK ROWLINSON

RYLAND
PETERS
& SMALL

LONDON NEW YORK

Ace A hole in one. Norman Manley, an amateur golfer from Long Beach, California, holds the record for the greatest number, an astonishing 59 of them!

Address The stance adopted before hitting the ball. Once the club has been grounded (or, in a hazard, the player has simply taken his stance), the ball is deemed to have been addressed, and if it moves thereafter (even if accidentally blown by the wind), it counts as a stroke.

Air shot A stroke that misses the ball, usually an uncontrolled swish by a beginner, but by no means always. "Just a practice swing," is the usual explanation.

Amateur A golfer who does not receive payment for playing. That seems simple enough, but 16 pages of *The Rules of Golf* are required to cover each and every potential loophole. You accept that hole-in-one prize of a car at your peril!

Apple Tree Gang Nickname for the small group of friends who began playing golf in a cow pasture at Yonkers, New York, in 1888. They are the founders of modern American golf (see Reid).

Apron To the golfer, an area of close-cut grass surrounding the putting surface. To the diner, what one hopes the kitchen staff wear.

Arison The British golf course architect C.H. Alison laid out several of the earliest and best courses in Japan. He was renowned for the inventiveness of his bunkering, influencing several subsequent generations of Japanese architects. Since his time, every deep bunker in Japan is known as an Alison, or "Arison," as the Japanese pronounce it.

Augusta National A very exclusive private club in Georgia founded by Bobby Jones (page 27). It is home to the Masters, the first Major of the golfing year.

Backspin The spectacular behavior of the golf ball on landing on a green after having been struck by a professional golfer who may spin the ball 15 or 20 feet or even more. The shot is still incomprehensible to most amateurs, yet in 1890 Sir Walter Simpson wrote in *Badminton Golf*, "Loft and backspin are the result of describing a small ellipse with the club." Simple!

Baffy A long-obsolete, lofted, wooden club used for approach work. Incredible as it may now seem, its function was similar to that of the modern wedge.

Ball Along with Harold Hilton (page 24) and Bobby Jones (page 27), John Ball (1861–1940) is one of only three amateurs to have won the Open Championship, to which he added no fewer than eight Amateur Championships. Such a tally is unlikely to be approached, let alone equalled.

Ballesteros The unique ability of Severiano Ballesteros (b. 1957) to fashion improbable rescue shots in his wild-hitting early days endeared him to galleries the world over and also won him his first Open Championship in 1979. With his good looks, dashing style, and magical improvisational skills, he became an international golfing icon and his victories in the Masters showed he could mix with the best at the highest level.

Baltusrol This is one of America's great championship courses, the name of which has a most unlikely provenance—it was named after a farmer, Baltus Roll, who was murdered here in 1831.

Bentgrass Today, a grass of the genus *Agrostis* found in many varieties and commonly used for fairway turf in northern Europe and the cooler parts of North America. Traditionally, in Scotland, it referred to a clump of tough grass in which the ball was very likely unplayable, and the shape of the shaft of the club after attempting a shot from it.

Bermudagrass Idyllic island with several handsome courses. Also a warm-climate grass that has made golf possible in the tropics.

Big Easy The nickname for the likeable South African, Ernie Els, whose majestic swing makes the game look ridiculously simple. A man of prodigious talents, he has won two US Opens as well as the 2002 Open Championship at Muirfield, Scotland.

Birdie A score of one under par on a particular hole, probably derived from a "bird," a fine shot that "flew like a bird." (Some sources suggest that the distinguished American course designer A.W. Tillinghast brought the word into common use through his articles in *Golf Illustrated*.)

Blind A blind shot is played over high ground to an unseen fairway or green. Such shots are generally avoided in modern golf course design and deplored by those who make their living from playing the game. Nevertheless, blind shots are considered by traditionalists to be an essential part of the sport and they declare that a blind hole is only blind once.

Bogey Nowadays a score of one over par on a hole, formerly the target score for a good amateur. The term is said to have originated at Great Yarmouth in England in the 1890s when Major Charles Wellman described the standard score of the course as "a regular Bogey Man." He was referring to the popular music-hall song, "Hush, hush, hush. Here comes the Bogey Man."

Braid James Braid (1870–1950) won the Open Championship five times between 1901 and 1910. A Scotsman, he won all his Opens on Scottish soil, which is slightly ironic given that he was a professional at English clubs, most notably Walton Heath, for most of his life (see Triumvirate).

Brassie Originally any wooden club fitted with a brass sole plate, but over time it became the name for a specific club halfway between a driver and a spoon (equivalent to the modern 2- or 3-wood).

Bunker A patch of sand which, on the earliest courses, was simply where the weather (or sheep sheltering from it) had eroded the natural seaside grasses. Today, bunkers are frequently elaborate sculptures in sand, prolifically dotted around the course to trap wayward shots. To the modern professional they present little hazard, that is until they encounter some of the deepest chasms of the great old links. In many parts of the world they are known as sand traps.

Caddie Derived from the French word meaning "younger son, army cadet," but by the 18th century, the term had been applied to a servant paid to carry golf clubs. Few amateur golfers today employ the services of a caddie, except at some of the more traditional clubs. However, a competent caddie is of inestimable value to the modern professional, acting not only as bag carrier and club cleaner, but also as an encyclopedia of yardages and borrows on the green, as well as a skilled counsellor.

Charleston The earliest American golf was almost certainly played in Charleston, South Carolina, in the 1740s, and a playing club was founded there in 1786. However, the introduction of golf to America is usually credited to John Reid (page 43) a century later.

Chip The shot most likely to show up the golfer who is short of practice. It is a low touch-shot that runs across the surface of the green toward the hole, requiring a delicate yet firm precision shot.

Choker A vitriolic description, all too frequently used by smug journalists, of a player who throws away victory by nervous play.

Cleek An iron club of former times usually (but not exclusively) with a narrow blade used for long approach shots. Putting cleeks were also not uncommon.

Colt Harry Shapland Colt (1869–1951) was one of the first golf course designers not to have been a professional golfer, and the first to create his designs on the drawing board. His many famous courses include Sunningdale and Wentworth.

Cotton Henry Cotton (1907–1987) restored pride and self-belief to British golf in the years either side of the Second World War when he stemmed the tide of American domination of the Open Championship by winning it three times—in 1934, 1937, and 1948. His construction of a golf course at Penina effectively sparked the golf boom in Portugal, the Algarve in particular.

Curtis Cup Biennial tournament between two teams of female amateur golfers representing the USA, and Great Britain and Ireland.

Darwin Bernard Darwin (1876–1961), grandson of the English naturalist Charles Darwin, was an amateur golfer of international standing. His greatest fame, however, was as one of the most perceptive and stylish of golf writers, the model for those who came after.

Demaret Jimmy Demaret (1910–1983) was one of the most colorful characters in American golf in the 1940s and 50s. He dressed flamboyantly and was an accomplished crooner, so accomplished, in fact, that it was not unknown for him to turn up to play golf still wearing his nightclub attire. It seemed to have little detrimental effect on his golf—he won three Masters.

Divot A piece of turf cut from the ground by the club in making a shot. Professionals always take their divot after striking the ball; beginners often take the divot first, in which case it may fly farther than the ball. Considerate golfers, professional or beginner, replace divots after every shot.

Dogleg A hole or fairway with a sharp turn, rather in the shape of a dog's hind leg. The extreme angles of some contemporary doglegs (dictated by real estate or boundary restrictions) suggest that the dog is in urgent need of a vet.

Dormie The pleasant state in match play of being in front by as many holes as there are left to be played. You cannot lose! (As long as there is no provision for extra holes, that is).

Downswing That part of the golf swing between the top of the backswing and impact where good golfers generate great clubhead speed. For many weekend golfers, downswing is the rapid reversal of fortune that almost inevitably follows an unusually well-played opening hole.

Driver Increasingly powerful clubs that propel the ball enormous distances from the tee. The combination of new "springy" driver faces and the latest ball technology is bringing previously unthought-of distances within the reach of even modest amateurs. As in motoring, erratic driving can bring disaster, yet the pros say, "Drive for show. Putt for dough."

Duffer An incompetent player, once the backbone of many a members' club, but these days mainly confined to social membership and the pages of P.G. Wodehouse, such is the scorn in which they are held by the club's tigers (page 53).

Dye Pete Dye (b. 1925) is the American golf course architect regarded by many as the *enfant terrible*. His trademark style is often summed up in pot bunkers and railroad ties, but that is to belittle his many challenging courses, such as TPC at Sawgrass, Harbour Town, and the Ocean Course at Kiawah Island.

Eagle A score of two under par on a hole, which is the expectation of every professional standing on the tee of a par 5 and an inconceivable prospect for all high handicappers.

Explosion A bunker shot in which a layer of sand is taken beneath the ball, the club not actually striking the ball itself. Good players use it to escape from steep-faced bunkers. Poor players simply get a face full of sand.

Fade A shot played with a slight left-to-right curve and the shape of shot preferred by many good professionals. For most also-rans it can easily degenerate into an uncontrollable slice, with the ball invariably disappearing into woods or over an out-of-bounds fence.

Faldo With three Masters titles and three Open Championship victories to his name, Nick Faldo (b. 1957) has been the most successful British golfer of modern times. He is unusual in that, for much of his professional career, he has employed a female caddie, Fanny Sunesson.

Featherie The old feather-stuffed, leather-covered ball, replaced by the much cheaper and more predictable gutta-percha ball from 1848. These handmade balls were expensive in their day and now fetch astronomical prices at auctions of golfing antiques.

Fescuegrass A grass found in cool climates, frequently encountered on old Scottish links courses. When it is well mown, it is an acceptable fairway grass; allowed to grow long and thick, it can be savage as rough.

"Fore!" The frequently heard cry the world over when a golfer has accidentally hit the ball toward someone else. It is a Scottish shortening of "before", meaning "ahead," in the sense of "Look out ahead!" Unfortunately, a poor example is being set these days by some of the world's top golfers who no longer bother to cry, "Fore!" when they hit their ball toward spectators.

Foursome A form of match play still popular at a few of the more traditional clubs in which each side consists of two players taking alternate strokes with a single ball. With intelligent play a foursome moves around the course very quickly, but it can easily test a friendship!

French Lick Not an entry in *The Joy of Sex*, but a charming old golf resort in Indiana, where Walter Hagen (page 23) won the 1924 US PGA Championship.

Fried egg An essential part of a hearty winter breakfast at many British golf clubs. Also an unenviable lie in a bunker, in which the ball is half-buried in the sand.

Furnace Creek The lowest golf course in the world at 214 feet (64 meters) below sea level, located in Death Valley, California.

Gallery Respectful name for the crowd of spectators watching a golf tournament. Most galleries are polite, knowledgeable and appreciative. Ridiculous shouts of "You're the man!" and "In the hole!," which accompany almost any shot by today's stars suggest there is a growing element of ignorance among those with better voice production than sense.

Golf widow A woman neglected by her golf-playing husband. There are no statistics available showing the proportion of golf widows to golf widowers.

Gorse An evergreen shrub (also called whin and furze) with yellow flowers and fearsome prickles, which grows profusely on many links courses in temperate areas. Trying to find a ball in it is usually a matter of extreme discomfort, the wiser option being the declaration of a lost ball.

Green committee A group of members charged with the maintenance and management of the course. Few committee members are properly equipped to undertake this work, with no formal training in greenkeeping, golf architecture, civil engineering, agronomy, or any of the other elements which fall under their charge, yet most do a decent job. Unfortunately, however, some of the "improvements" made to classic courses over the years have been little short of painting moustaches on the Mona Lisa.

Greensome An informal, player-friendly sort of four-ball competition in which everyone plays a tee shot on each hole. One ball from each team is chosen, and play continues thereafter with alternate shots.

Gross The full score made before deduction (or addition) of handicap. A score approaching a gross suggests that a few lessons might be prudent.

Hacker An unskillful player, the great majority of golfers. Also, possibly that rare bird who is able to get into the club computer to massage his handicap.

Hagen Walter Hagen (1892–1969)) was the larger-than-life American golfer who refused to be treated like dirt simply because he was a professional player. As a result, his fellow professionals rose from pitiful earnings and inferior status to considerable wealth and public adoration. Supremely confident, he was the impressive winner of four Open Championships, two US Opens, and five US PGAs—these last all the more remarkable because the PGA was a knockout tournament in his day. He thrived on his playboy image, yet it was he who told us, "Don't forget to smell the flowers along the way."

Handicap Strokes deducted from the scores of less talented players to enable them to compete on (fairly) even terms. In general, handicaps reflect a player's competence, but the system is open to abuse by pot hunters (page 41).

Hanging lie A downhill lie, with the ball often played below the level of the feet that generally makes for a difficult shot, particularly disliked by high-handicappers, who will frequently top the ball or slice it.

Hazard Exactly what it says it is: any obstruction such as a bunker, stream, lake, or pond providing a strategic obstacle to the player. Special rules cover play from such inhospitable spots and the relief which may be sought from them (under penalty, of course).

Hickory The North American timber used for making the shafts of the best golf clubs until the advent of steel shafts in the 1920s.

Hilton Like his great rival John Ball (page 8), Harold Hilton (1869–1942), learned his golf on the Royal Liverpool links at Hoylake. As an amateur he beat distinguished fields of professionals to win two Open Championships, a feat exceeded only by the extraordinary Bobby Jones (page 27).

Hogan Ben Hogan (1912–1997) is one of only five players to have won the Grand Slam of all four Major trophies. He won two US PGAs and a US Open shortly after the Second World War, but in 1949 he was involved in a car crash. So seriously was he injured that it was thought he would never be able to walk again. However, with his indomitable courage and dogged determination, he went on to take three more US Opens, two Masters titles, and an Open Championship.

Honourable Company of Edinburgh Golfers The distinguished Scottish golf club founded in 1744, which gave us the first set of rules. Its course at Muirfield is a regular Open Championship venue.

Hooker Neither a woman of easy virtue nor a rugby forward, but a golfer who habitually curves shots from right to left. In theory, a ball flies farther with a touch of draw, but it is a hard shot to control consistently.

Inverness The distinguished club at Toledo, Ohio, host to many Majors, which was the first to welcome professionals into the clubhouse. This it did for the first time during the 1920 US Open Championship.

Iron A club which in the past was made of iron. Today they are more usually made of steel, bronze, or more exotic metals.

Jacklin Tony Jacklin (b. 1944) revitalized British golf with his short reign at the top of the ladder from 1969 to 1972. For a brief period he was Open Champion of both Britain and the USA. As a Ryder Cup captain he inspired his European team to great feats. Such success took its toll on Jacklin's sensitive personality, but the next generation of European stars owed much to him.

Japan A golf-crazy country where golf courses are few and phenomenally expensive. It is said to be cheaper to fly to Europe, stay in a prestigious hotel and play a top course, than it is to play a single round on many Japanese courses.

Jersey School This tiny island in the English Channel with a population well short of six figures produced several of the dominant players in world golf in the late 19th and early 20th centuries. Harry Vardon (page 56) and Ted Ray head the list, but there were two more Vardons, two Gaudins, and T.G. Renouf, all of whom were golfers of international standing.

Jigger A moderately lofted, shallow-faced iron club used for approach shots that is no longer in use. It is also the name of a small glass (usually for serving whisky). A full bottle of Scotch fills 18 jiggers—one per hole.

Jones Robert Trent Jones (1906–2000) was a prolific American golf course architect who built 310 courses and remodelled 150 others in a career that lasted 70 years. His courses have been the setting for 20 US Opens, 12 US PGA Championships, and 47 other national championships—an unequalled record.

Jones Robert Tyre Jones (Bobby) (1902–1971) was an amateur golfer who competed against the finest professionals of the day to win four US Opens and three Open Championships. He also won five US Amateurs and one British, including all four championships in 1930 (see Quadrilateral). He retired from competitive golf at the tender age of 28! Subsequently he developed the Augusta National golf course and Masters tournament. In later life he suffered from a crippling spinal disease. His dignity was summed up by Herbert Warren Wind: "As a young man, he was able to stand up to just about the best that life can offer, which is not easy, and later he stood up with equal grace to just about the worst."

Kick An unpredictable bounce on landing, loathed by most professionals and those brought up on impeccably manicured inland courses. Considered sporting by traditional links golfers.

Lag Refers to putting and is one of the most impressive features of many professionals' game. It is the considerable art of leaving long putts no more than a pace from the hole, thereby ensuring the next putt is a guaranteed tap-in.

Langer Bernhard Langer (b. 1957), a man of deep religious conviction, has proved to be the most enduring of the European stars who emerged in the wake of Ballesteros (page 8). Twice a Masters champion, he has overcome several bouts of the dreaded yips (page 62), unique at his level of golf.

Lay up To play deliberately short, either to leave a full shot subsequently or to avoid a hazard. Rarely seen among higher handicappers, who will almost invariably go for the impossible shot, usually with disastrous consequences.

Lefties Unlike in most other sports, there are and have been very few left-handed golfers of any quality. Until Mike Weir took the 2003 Masters, only New Zealander Bob Charles had ever won a Major (the 1968 Open Championship). Some would say that the talented American Phil Mickelson is the finest current left-handed golfer not to have won a Major. It is slightly strange as more of the work in a golf shot is done by the top hand and for a lefty that is the right (and usually stronger) hand.

Lie In golfing terms, where the ball has come to rest. A bad lie being, for example, in a clump of long grass rather than a transparent fib.

Links Derived from old Scottish and English words meaning ridges or hummocks, a links is traditionally a sandy, treeless, undulating area, often with dunes and gorse bushes and usually close to the sea. The natural turf is of bent- and fescuegrasses, giving tight lies and demanding crisp ball striking.

Lip The edge of the golf hole. Lipping out being the infuriating habit of many a putt to run around the rim of the hole before failing to drop into the cup. Also, the verbal abuse given by a professional golfer to the spectator who makes a distracting noise during the player's swing.

Locke Arthur d'Arcy Locke (1917–1987), known as Bobby in the golfing world, was the South African golfer who defied perceived wisdom by playing all his golf with a pronounced draw, (even his putts were hit with a slight right-to-left motion). But it was a sound enough technique to bring him four Open titles and 11 US Tour titles in the days when few foreigners could compete successfully against the best Americans.

Loft The amount by which a club face is laid back in order to get the ball airborne.

Longhurst With his relaxed yet perceptive style, Henry Longhurst (1909–1978) became the first British TV golf commentator to achieve equal fame across the Atlantic.

Macdonald Charles Blair Macdonald (1856–1939) won the first official US Amateur Championship in 1895. His cavalier attitude to two earlier attempts to set up a national championship was indirectly responsible for the establishment of the United States Golf Association (USGA). Having learned the game in Scotland and studied its courses in minute detail, he went on to be the first great and influential American-born course designer, with his National Golf Links reckoned to be the country's first great course.

Mackenzie Alister Mackenzie (1870–1934) was a Leeds doctor who gave up medicine for golf-course design. While serving in the Boer War, he learned the skills of military camouflage, an art he later put to deceptive use in his new career. He served as a camouflage expert in the First World War and is credited by Marshal Foch with having saved more lives through this than anybody else in the war. His best course designs include Cypress Point and Augusta National.

Majors The most coveted trophies in the sport: the Masters, US Open, Open Championship, and US PGA. To date, only five players have won all four trophies: Gene Sarazen, Ben Hogan, Gary Player, Jack Nicklaus, and Tiger Woods. Only Woods has managed to hold all four at the same time, albeit briefly.

Mary The first woman golfer to be mentioned by name was Mary, Queen of Scots. She was playing golf at Seton when she was told of the death of her husband, Lord Darnley. Her apparent lack of concern was cited during the trial which led to her execution in 1587.

Mashie One of the most useful clubs in the bag in the days when clubs had names, not numbers. It was a lofted club used for pitching to the green, its name being derived from the Scottish word "mash," meaning sledgehammer.

Masters The first Major of the professional golfing year, the only Major to be held on the same course (Augusta National) every year, and the only Major to be an invitational event.

Match In matchplay, the original form of golf, the contest is decided by the number of holes won rather than the total number of strokes taken.

Morris The two Toms, Old and Young, father and son, were the dominant players of the mid-19th century, capturing eight Open Championships between them. Tom Senior became one of the earliest golf course architects, with brilliant Muirfield and stunning Royal County Down to his name.

Mulligan A free shot that many Americans award themselves when their opening drive disappears out of bounds. In the rest of the world it is simply "three off the tee."

Musselburgh Located in Scotland, this is the oldest playing course in the world (1672), and was host to six early Opens. It's an inexpensive public course open to all comers and has hickory-shafted clubs available for rent by those who want to emulate the deeds of the great Victorian players.

Myopia Hunt Club Surely the strangest-named club ever to host the US Open, which it did four times between 1898 and 1908. Several founding members, including the four sons of Boston Mayor Frederick Prince, were near-sighted baseball players who always wore glasses. They gave their nickname, The Myopia Nine, to the new club.

Nassau A popular form of bet on the outcome of a round of golf with an equal stake wagered on the front nine, back nine, and the match as a whole.

Nelson The swing of Byron Nelson (b. 1940) was so consistent that the USGA's ball-testing machine is called the Iron Byron. It took him to two Masters, one US Open, and two US PGA titles. But his most remarkable feat was winning 18 of the 30 US Tour events he entered in 1945, coming second in a further seven, and never finishing worse than ninth. Included in that was a phenomenal streak of 11 consecutive tournament victories.

"Never up, never in" The traditional phrase describing a weak, short putt. It is usually uttered in English wherever in the world golf is played.

Niblick An obsolete club, thought to be derived from "short nose." It was steeply lofted and used for getting out of tricky situations such as deep rough.

Nicklaus Jack Nicklaus (b. 1940) is statistically the greatest achiever in golf history, with 18 Majors to his name (three Open Championships, four US Opens, five US PGAs, and six Masters) plus two US Amateurs. So impressive were his gifts that Bobby Jones said that he "played a game with which I am not familiar." In victory he was majestic, yet he was always a dignified and generous loser. Known as the Golden Bear, Nicklaus was famous (and feared) for his last round charges, not least when he won the Masters in 1986 at the age of 46 by playing the last ten holes in 7 under par.

Nineteenth The universal euphemism for the bar and its soothing tinctures.

Norman One of golf's unluckiest players, having lost four Majors in play-offs and come second in countless others, Greg Norman (b. 1955) remains one of the most popular golfers in the sport, with dashing good looks, a swing to die for, and broad smiles to the galleries even in adversity. With two Open victories and 75 victories in other tournaments, he is one of the wealthiest men in golf.

Oakmont Possibly the toughest golf course in the world, even though it no longer boasts the 220 bunkers it once had! See also Pine Valley.

Old Course Many clubs with more than one course have an Old Course, but *the* Old Course, famous throughout the world, is that at St. Andrews.

One-iron The longest and least-lofted iron club, rarely carried even by today's professionals. It is hard to hit successfully, so difficult that Lee Trevino (page 54) once quipped that you could safely hold up a 1-iron in a thunderstorm, "Even God can't hit a 1-iron!"

Ontario National Not, as you might imagine, a golf course in Canada, but a public links a few miles east of Los Angeles.

Open Championship The senior Major, with a history dating back to 1860 when Willie Park won at Prestwick. Having won the original trophy, The Belt, three times in succession, Tom Morris Junior (page 34) was allowed to keep it in 1870. The first competition for the current trophy, The Claret Jug, was held in 1872, when young Morris triumphed yet again.

Palmer With his dashing, cavalier style, and winning personality, Arnold Palmer (b. 1929) was the first golfing idol of the American TV audience. He also put the Open Championship back on the world golf calendar, persuading his compatriots that they should make the pilgrimage to Britain. His career at the very top was remarkably short, 1958–1964, but in that time he collected four Masters titles, one US Open, and two Opens. Now retired, he lives at Bay Hill in Florida, where he is the moving force behind the club and its annual US Tour Invitational.

Par A standard score based on the theoretical play of a first-class golfer. According to the length of the hole, either one, two, or three shots are allowed to reach the green, and two putts are assumed. Holes up to 250 yards are, therefore, par 3s; holes between 251 and 475 yards par 4s, and over 475 yards they are par 5s. However, the prodigious play of contemporary professionals has seen the advent of 500-yard par 4s. Par for the course, then, is the total of the individual pars for each hole, usually being between 68 and 73. Unfortunately, many courses are "tricked up" for championships to ensure the winning score is not significantly under par. Par is a silly god, but an admirable way of comparing players' scores when they are on different holes.

Pau The earliest course in Continental Europe was established in 1856 in this elegant French town at the foot of the Pyrenees by a group of British ex-pats. They also introduced fox hunting and steeplechasing to the region.

Persimmon This is a tree of the genus *Diospyros* whose hard wood was used to make the finest handcrafted drivers and fairway woods until the advent of the more forgiving metal woods.

Pine Valley The other contender (along with Oakmont, page 38) for the title of the toughest golf course in the world. If you are not on the fairway or green, you are almost certainly lost in dense forest or in the water, or else you are fighting to escape the vast expanses of sand — not so much a profusion of bunkers as a continuous 184-acre bunker!

Player The South African Gary Player (b. 1935) was (with Palmer and Nicklaus) one of golf's Big Three—winning nine Majors between 1959 and 1978 and becoming one of only five players to hold the Grand Slam of one each of all the Majors. His tenacity, indomitable spirit, religious faith, and incredible fitness kept him remarkably competitive into his 60s.

Plus fours Baggy trousers, known as knickerbockers or knickers in the USA, that were particularly popular with golfers in the inter-war years. The overhang of 4 inches (10 cm) of material below the knees (hence the name) allowed the golfer notable freedom of movement.

Pot hunters Golfers who contrive (by bad play) to maintain an artificially high handicap at their home club in order to win trophies at other clubs.

Prestwick An ancient Scottish golf links which was host to the very first Open Championship in 1860 and a further 23 after that. The course has altered since then, but it remains a classic of period golf.

Public links Golf courses, often municipally owned, open to the general public for a modest green fee. Many look on them as being somewhat inferior, but the Black Course at Bethpage State Park was good enough to host the 2002 US Open Championship.

Quadrilateral The Impregnable Quadrilateral was the term given to Bobby Jones's remarkable feat of 1930 when he won the Open and Amateur Championships of both Britain and the USA in one astonishing season.

Quail-high Charming American description of a ball hit on a low and flat trajectory (often to keep below the branches of a tree or to minimize the effects of a strong wind).

Rabbit The mammalian scourge of many a golf club, digging unwelcome holes in beautifully manicured fairways and greens. Also an affectionate, if slightly disparaging, term for a golfer with little or no ability.

Rake Golfer who drives to the club in a flashy car and insists his pretty blonde companion walks with him around the course to admire his exploits. Also an implement for smoothing out the humps and bumps left in a bunker after a golfer has played from it. A rake was also a curious iron club, no longer in use, with a number of prongs instead of a solid face, which was apparently very effective at getting the ball out of water or fluffy sand.

Read Good golfers "read" greens, revealing all the contours of the putting surface. The rest of us look from every angle, hold our putters vertically like a plumb line, and don't understand why our putts still fail to finish within a mile of the hole.

Redan The famous short 15th at North Berwick on the Scottish coast is golf's most copied hole, reproduced on courses the world over. However, few imitations capture the subtlety of the original, which offers several playing options depending on the wind, pin position, and player's skill.

Reid John Reid (1840–1916) is the father of American golf. He is the man who, with other members of the Apple Tree Gang (page 6), effectively introduced golf as we know it to the USA.

Ross The founder of American golf course design, Scotsman Donald Ross (1872–1948) migrated from Dornoch in 1898 taking with him a thorough knowledge of the special features of Scotland's finest old courses. He was a prolific designer, his style retaining a Scottish links feel, and his cunningly raised greens remain stringent tests of the approach shot.

R & A The standard abbreviation for the Royal and Ancient Golf Club, located in St. Andrews, Scotland, overlooking the 18th green of The Old Course. It is the official rules body for the game of golf throughout most of the world, apart from North America. It also stages such events as the Walker Cup, Open Championship, and Amateur Championship. Contrary to popular belief, it doesn't own the golf courses at St. Andrews, which are in fact owned by the municipal borough and run by the St. Andrews Links Trust.

Royal Calcutta The oldest golf club in the world outside the British Isles. It was founded as the Dum Dum Golfing Club in 1829.

Royal County Down One of the world's great courses laid out for the princely sum of £4 (just under US $8) by Old Tom Morris in 1889.

Royal Melbourne The West Course at Royal Melbourne is judged by many to be Australia's finest and among the top ten in the world.

Royal Montreal Founded in 1873, Royal Montreal is the first properly established golf club on the American continent.

Rub of the green A quaint term describing an accident to the ball not caused by the player, such as being inadvertently stopped by a passerby or deflected by hitting a stone. Generally speaking the ball must be played from where it has come to rest, but in some countries there are local rules giving relief when a ball comes to rest beside, say, an alligator or rattlesnake.

Ryder Sam Ryder (1858–1936) was a wealthy seed merchant who inaugurated a competition which took place every two years between teams of professional golfers representing the USA, and Great Britain and Ireland. After many years of very one-sided encounters, the format of the Ryder Cup was changed to the USA versus Europe, and each contest since then has been enthralling.

Rye A wonderful, if very private, links course on the south coast of England, home to the Oxford and Cambridge Golfing Society. It is also a hard-wearing variety of grass frequently encountered on golf courses throughout the world, except in places with extreme heat or humidity.

St. Andrews Known as the "home of golf," the ancient university town of St. Andrews has played host to the game certainly since 1552, but most probably for several centuries before that. Its influence on the development of the game worldwide began in 1754 when the Royal and Ancient Golf Club (R & A) was founded. There are currently nine courses in and around the town.

Sarazen See Squire.

Schenectady A town in New York which gave its name to an early center-shafted putter with an aluminum head. Walter Travis used one to win the British Amateur Championship in 1904, whereupon the Royal and Ancient Golf Club immediately banned its use.

Scratch A zero handicap, the word coming from the mark on the ground from where the best runner started in a handicap race. Hence the term, "starting from scratch."

Shank Probably the most destructive shot in golf in which the ball is struck by the hosel of the club, making it squirt off almost at right angles to the intended direction. The results can be devastating and seriously undermine the player's confidence. Sam Snead described shanks as, "So contagious that even watching them is risky."

Simpson Englishman Tom Simpson (1877–1964) designed some of France and Belgium's finest courses, but it was his eccentricity that made him one of the most intriguing characters in the world of golf during the inter-war years. A wealthy man, he was chauffeur-driven in his Rolls-Royce to meet potential clients, dressed in a cloak and beret. It is reputed that Simpson ordered his chauffeur to drive round and round the meeting room when one of his designs was being considered, not letting the occupants leave until they had agreed to his bid. Fortunately, his courses were of considerable quality.

Singh   Fiji's Vijay Singh (b. 1963) has been one of the most consistent of all the world's golfers of the past decade. An obsessive practiser, he won the 1998 US PGA and 2000 US Masters and is rarely far from contention in any tournament he enters. Four wins on the 2003 US PGA Tour helped him to his first Tour money title, thereby winning the prestigious Arnold Palmer Award.

Snead   Sam Snead (1912–2002) came from the backwoods of Virginia. Using probably the most natural swing ever seen in the game, he won three Masters, three US PGAs, and one Open Championship. He won professional tournaments over a period of six decades, from 1936 to 1982, and was the oldest winner of a US Tour event aged 52.

Solheim Cup   The most recent of the transatlantic challenges, a biennial contest between the professional women golfers of Europe and the USA.

Sorenstam   The Swedish golfer, Annika Sorenstam (b. 1970), has been the dominant player in women's golf since 1995 when she first triumphed in the US Women's Open despite the strongest efforts of some very capable opposition. She made history in 2003 by playing in the Colonial tournament on the men's tour.

Spoon   Originally any club with a concave head resembling the bowl of a spoon. In time, the term was applied to a wooden club, a little more lofted than a brassie (page 12), equivalent to a 3- or 4-wood.

Squire The Squire was the nickname of Gene Sarazen (1902–1999), the diminutive and much-loved American golfer who was the first player to achieve the Grand Slam—victories in the four Majors: the Open Championship, US Open, US PGA, and the Masters. He also invented the sand wedge, which revolutionized bunker play and for which we should all be very thankful.

Stableford A form of stroke play invented by Dr. Frank Stableford, particularly popular with golfing societies in Britain, in which points are scored in relation to par. Stableford was a member of Wallasey Golf Club in England.

Stymie A situation on the putting green in which one player's ball blocks the line of another player's to the hole, which was abolished in 1951. However, the word is still used in the English language to mean thwart or hinder, even by many who have never played golf.

Sudden death A form of play-off used to find a winner of a tournament when two or more players have tied for the lead. The implication is that golfers who fall by the wayside suffer sudden death, rather than the winner enjoying sudden victory.

Sweet spot That particular spot on the clubface off which the ball flies perfectly. Persimmon woods and old bladed irons had tiny sweet spots in comparison with today's metal woods and cavity-backed irons, and required much greater precision of strike.

Takeaway The teaching professional's word for the backswing.

Taylor J.H. Taylor (1871–1963) was the first Englishman to win the Open Championship on English soil in 1894, when Royal St. George's became the first club outside Scotland to host the event. (See Triumvirate).

Tee A wooden or plastic peg on which the ball is placed for driving. In the early days of the game of golf, a small heap of sand or mud was used for this purpose. Tee also refers to the teeing ground, the starting place from which the hole is played.

Thomson Australian Peter Thomson (b. 1929) was a five-times Open Champion. He was one of the masters of controlling the smaller British ball then in use in testing seaside conditions. He did much to develop the game of golf in Asia and Africa, and continues to run a flourishing course design practice.

Three-putt Almost a criminal offense for professional golfers who will drop a shot to par by so doing. For the weekend hacker three-putt territory starts about two paces from the hole.

Threesome A form of match very rarely encountered in which one golfer plays against two, the two taking alternate shots with a single ball. It can be fun.

Through the green Basically, anywhere on the golf course other than teeing grounds, putting greens and hazards, and not simply, as might be imagined, off the back of the putting surface.

Tiger A brilliant golfer with prodigious ability—a term used for many years before the advent of Tiger Woods (page 61).

Tillie Albert Warren Tillinghast (1874–1942) is said to have introduced the word "birdie" to the golfing dictionary. He was also the designer of many of America's finest courses, including Winged Foot and San Francisco Golf Club.

Touch Delicate and sensitive control of testing little shots on and around the green. It has been remarkable that many of the game's most powerful hitters, such as Jack Nicklaus, John Daly, and Tiger Woods, have also had the most refined of touches.

TPC Tournament Players' Club, a series of "stadium" courses constructed throughout the USA primarily for the playing of professional tournaments, offering spectators unrivalled viewing and considerable spectacle. The TPC at Sawgrass hosts the annual Players' Championship, considered by some as the fifth Major.

Track iron A very old club, long obsolete, used to play balls lying in cart tracks, hoof prints, and other awkward lies that were commonly found on early golf courses.

Trap The customary American term for what the British call a bunker. Either way they are more feared by amateurs than professionals.

Trevino Lee Trevino (b. 1939) came from the US/Mexican border and learned golf by playing with a broken bottle. Supermex, as he was known, had an unorthodox swing, hitting the ball with a persistent slice, yet he broke through by winning the 1968 US Open. He won again in 1971, took two Open Championships, and also two US PGAs. His fast wit made him a favorite with the crowds, but underneath this flippant exterior was a man of steel.

Triumvirate James Braid, J.H. Taylor, and Harry Vardon make up the Great Triumvirate who dominated the Open Championship from 1894 to 1914. Between them they won it no fewer than 16 times (five each to Braid and Taylor and a record six for Vardon.)

Tuctu The highest golf course in the world is Tuctu GC in Peru at an altitude of 14,335 feet (4,369 meters).

Unplayable The term used to describe a ball when it lies in such an awkward spot that the player may have no possible shot, or that it is simply not worth trying to play the ball as it lies. Under the rules of golf, relief may be obtained under penalty and, unusually, the player himself is the sole judge of whether or not the ball is unplayable. He does not need to consult anyone else.

Up and down The playing of a deft rescue shot from off the green or in a bunker, followed by a single putt to rescue par—commonplace in professional golf, a near miracle for most amateurs. Such a combination of shots played from a bunker is usually referred to as a "sand save."

USGA The United States Golf Association is the governing body of golf in the USA—the American counterpart of the Royal and Ancient Golf Club of St. Andrews in the UK.

US Open The second most senior Major, begun in 1894 at St. Andrews, New York. The first tournament was decided by matchplay, but from 1895 it has been a stroke-play competition. Bobby Jones, Ben Hogan, and Jack Nicklaus share the record for the number of wins, each winning four times.

US PGA Championship Often considered the bridesmaid of the Majors, the US Professional Golfers' Association Championship has been contested since 1916. For many years it was a matchplay competition, which makes Walter Hagen's tally of five victories quite remarkable. In 1958 the format changed to strokeplay, with Jack Nicklaus equalling Hagen's record in 1980.

Van de Velde There are few golfers who lose a tournament in such a bizarre fashion that the public remembers him rather than the winner. The attractive Frenchman, Jean Van de Velde (b. 1966), seemed to have the 1999 Open Championship in the bag, but a series of catastrophic shots on Carnoustie's formidable 18th, including a pitiful skirmish with the Barry Burn, turned his victory march into pure slapstick. He ran up a triple-bogey 7 to fritter away his lead putting him in a three-way play-off, which was comfortably won by Scotland's Paul Lawrie.

Vardon Harry Vardon (1870–1937) won six Open Championships between 1896 and 1914 (a record still unequalled). He popularized the overlapping grip that bears his name, although it was actually invented by J.E. Laidlay.

Vicenzo By the time Roberto de Vicenzo (b. 1923) retired from top-level golf, he was reckoned to have won 240 tournaments with pride of place going to his 1967 Open Championship victory. However, he is remembered, unhappily, for signing an incorrect card in the 1968 Masters. He appeared to have tied for the lead with Bob Goalby, but by signing for a four at the 17th instead of a three, he was deemed to have lost by a stroke. As in life, Vicenzo displayed notable dignity at this awful moment.

Walk While some would say that golf is a good walk spoiled, others would say that golf is spoiled by not walking. Some traditional clubs (mostly British) only sanction the use of golf carts to those with an appropriate medical certificate.

Walker Cup A biennial tournament played between two teams of male amateur golfers representing the USA, and Great Britain and Northern Ireland.

Water clubs These clubs, specially designed to play the ball out of water, were much in vogue in the late 19th and early 20th centuries. Most of them featured holes punched in the blade of the club, and all are now illegal.

Watson For a few years in the 1970s and 80s, Tom Watson (b. 1949) was the brightest star in the firmament, winning five Open Championships, two Masters, and a US Open. It was the manner of his wins which so impressed, not least the "Duel in the Sun" shootout between him and Nicklaus in the Open Championship at Turnberry in 1977, which to many was the greatest Open of them all. Watson is now enjoying a successful career on the Seniors' Tour.

Wethered Joyce Wethered (1899–1997), or Lady Heathcoat-Amory as she became, was one of the greatest amateur golfers of either sex in the inter-war years. Bobby Jones was moved to say that he had, "never played golf with anyone, man or woman, amateur or professional, who made me feel so utterly outclassed."

Whipping Not what the in-form player gives the rabbit (see page 42), but the thread binding the head of a wooden club to the shaft, redundant since the advent of metal woods.

Who? Ben Who? was the nickname given to Ben Curtis (b. 1977), the journeyman American of whom few had heard, who surprised everybody by playing sound enough golf to win the Open Championship at Sandwich in 2003. Against all expectations, the big names around him fell away and failed to catch him.

Winter rules Local rules allowing the moving of the ball to a more favorable lie in winter conditions, nominally to help protect the course from damage. According to *Newsweek*, President Nixon played "'winter rules' year-round, moving his ball to favorable lies and ignoring the two-stroke penalty for out-of-bounds infractions." This is useful information for those who regularly play golf with American Presidents.

Woods Tiger Woods (b. 1975) is the best player in the world at the start of the 21st century, some would say of all time—time will tell. His winner's speeches and his way with journalists suggest that if ever he tires of golf, there is a distinguished career ahead as a diplomat.

Woods Large-headed clubs for long shots made of steel, titanium, tungsten, graphite, and space-rocket materials, but never nowadays made of wood.

X-out Reject balls sold at bargain basement prices. Don't expect consistent performance, but they are just the thing for the wayward hacker who expects to lose a few on every round.

Yards Despite the inexorable march of metrication throughout the world, yards are still used to measure golf holes and courses in the UK, North America, and to some extent in Japan. In theory there is little difference between one meter and one yard, but a 9-iron might carry onto a green 120 yards way, but may well finish in a green-front bunker or lake on a 120-meter hole—a difference of ten feet (or three meters).

Yips The dreaded putting affliction that makes golfers unable to take the club back from address. Almost like an addiction, "Once you've got 'em you've always got 'em." The German golfer Bernhard Langer is probably the only world-class player who has managed to combat the yips successfully—three times, in fact.

Zaharias "Babe" Zaharias (1915–1956) was a star athlete of the 1932 Olympic Games, during which she set three world records. When her athletics career came to an end, she took up golf, first as an amateur—winning the US and British Amateur Women's Championships—then as one of the earliest women tour professionals. Her glittering career was crowned by three US Women's Open titles.

Zoeller In 1979, Frank Urban (Fuzzy) Zoeller (b. 1951) became the first golfer in modern times to win the Masters at his first attempt. His victory in the 1984 US Open proved that this was no fluke.

Zoysiagrass A coarse-bladed grass suitable for the extreme climatic changes of parts of the USA and Japan (where it is known as *korai*). The ball sits up and flies well from it.

CREDITS

All photography by Dan Duchars with the exception of:

Front jacket golf ball image Peter Dazeley, London

Page 14 © copyright Photolibrary.com

Senior Designer Paul Tilby
Editor Sharon Ashman
Picture Research Claire Hector
Production Patricia Harrington
Art Director Gabriella Le Grazie
Publishing Director Alison Starling

First published in the USA in 2004
by Ryland Peters & Small, Inc.
519 Broadway, 5th Floor
New York, NY 10012
www.rylandpeters.com

Text, design, and commissioned photographs
© copyright Ryland Peters & Small 2004

10 9 8 7 6 5 4 3 2 1

ISBN 1 84172 727 X

Printed in China